Magnificent Monuments of India

The Kailash Temple at Ellora

Great Art in Stone

Tilottama Shome

Illustrated by Kavita Singh Kale

talking CUB
An Imprint of Speaking Tiger Books

TALKING CUB

125A, Ground Floor, Shahpur Jat,
Near Asiad Village, New Delhi - 110 049

First published in paperback in Talking Cub
by Speaking Tiger Books in 2022

The illustrations are artistic representation and not to scale.

Every effort has been made to trace individual copyright holders of photographs and obtain permission. Any omission brought to our attention will be remedied in the future.

Book design by Maithili Doshi Aphale

ISBN: 978-93-5447-147-6

eISBN: 978-93-5447-155-1

10 9 8 7 6 5 4 3 2 1

Typeset in Cardo by Jojy Philip
Printed at SBM Industries Pvt Ltd, Rai (www.sbmprints.com)

To the unknown sculptors whose hands and
tools carved rock into monuments.
To my daughters who have trailed me in my adventures
with curiosity but without questioning the adult.

Contents

The Temples on the Hills

It was autumn but the sun was scorching hot. My car was weaving its way up the Sahyadri hills which are part of the Western Ghats in Maharashtra. A citadel sat atop a hillock in the distance. Those were the walls of the Daulatabad Fort, built in the 12th century CE by a Yadav general, Raja Billamraj. My history book said that the fort was later taken over by the Sultans of Delhi and Mohammed bin Tughlaq, an eccentric ruler of the Delhi Sultanate, had moved his capital to this fort.

The countryside I was passing through was dotted with old ruins. Ramparts of the fort, partly crumbling, seemed to stand by, quietly witnessing the changing times. Whenever I drive past old ruins and citadels, I always wonder—if someone were to ask the piles of stone to relate all that they have witnessed over centuries, what would their response be?

I was on my way to see the Ellora Caves, located on the outskirts of the city of Aurangabad in Maharashtra. Aurangabad gets its name from Emperor Aurangzeb, the last of the Great Mughals, who lived and ruled from this city in

◆ *Daulatabad Fort*

the 17th century. His simple, almost bare tomb, open to the sky, can be seen even today. I had already visited the tomb, and now I was going to step back another 1500 years, to the caves of Ellora. The caves are located almost around the corner from the Mughal king's grave. So just by travelling a few kilometres more, I was about to witness how Indian art and architecture had changed over 2000 years.

I asked my driver how far we were from Ellora and he said, in the typical relaxed style of the people of the area, 'Bas, we are about to reach soon.'

I opened the book I had been reading, eager to quickly remind myself about the story of Ellora and of this region.

◆ *Aurangzeb's tomb*

A Story of Kings and Vassals

The Ellora caves were built over a period of time—from the 6th century CE to the 10th century CE. Historians say that there were three building periods—an early Hindu period (550 to 600 CE), a Buddhist phase (600 to 730 CE) and a later Hindu and Jain phase (730 to 950 CE). The caves at Ellora were built by various rulers but the Rashtrakutas were the main dynasty who seem to have built many of the caves.

Occupying a rocky area in the Western Ghats, the caves have been carved out of volcanic basalt. Basalt is a type of rock that is formed when lava cools. It is a very hardy rock and in fact, the word basalt means 'very hard stone' in Latin.

As I approached Ellora, I could see the mildly hilly terrain was covered with lush green trees and shrubs. The monsoons had helped paint the landscape green. My thoughts wandered back in time again…

My time-turner history book said that the grandest of the caves at Ellora was Kailash, built in the 8th century CE. What did the map of the Indian subcontinent look like at that time? The Rashtrakuta dynasty was ruling over today's Karnataka and Maharashtra. They had built their empire with the Gulbarga region in modern Karnataka as its base. In the east,

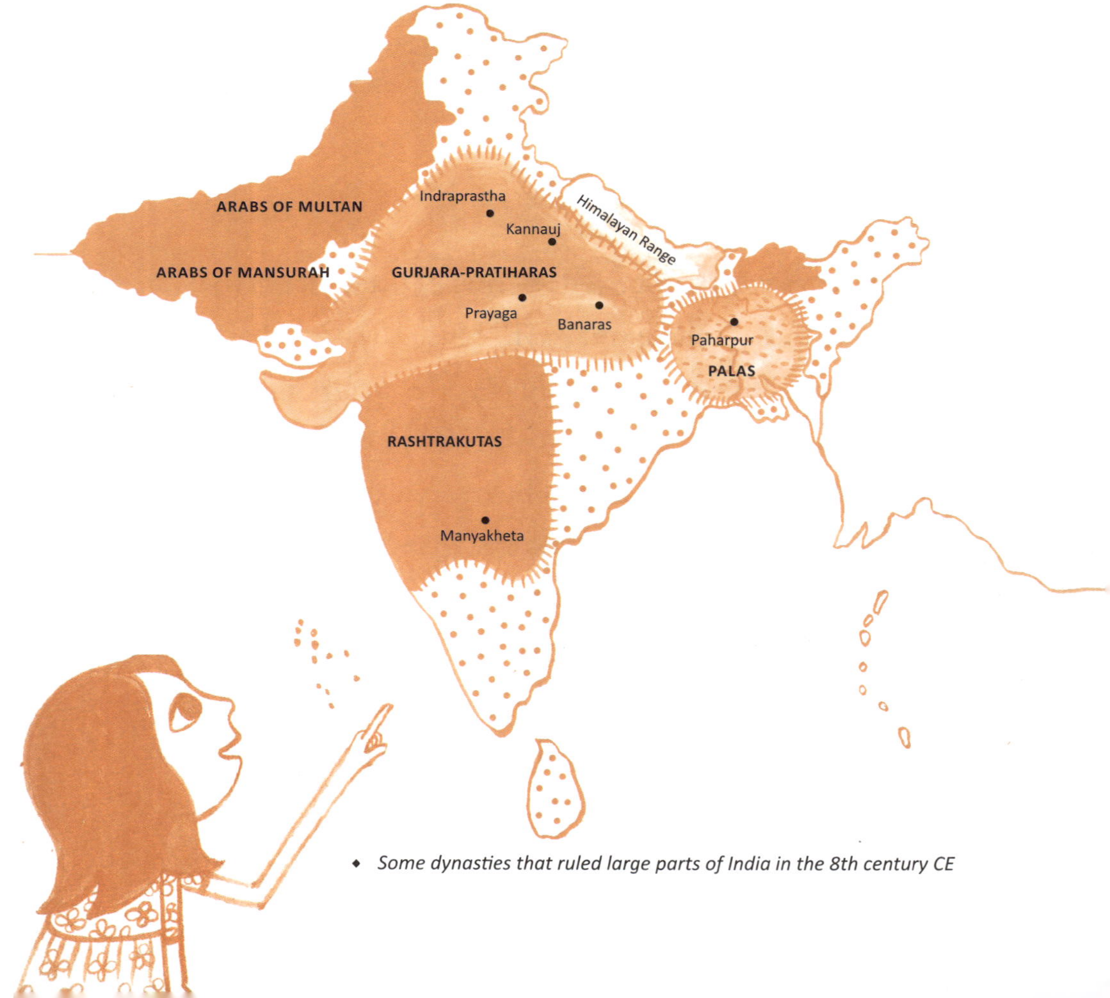

Some dynasties that ruled large parts of India in the 8th century CE

the Palas were gaining power, and the Prathihara dynasty was flourishing in the north-west.

A large part of Ellora was built under Rashtrakuta rule. This dynasty was one of warriors, yet they were also generous patrons of scholars in a variety of subjects. Language, mathematics and the arts were some areas that were patronized by the Rashtrakuta kings. They were also very interested in architecture and this is probably why such fabulous monuments like the Kailash Temple at Ellora were built during their rule.

Every dynasty has its own stories and legends. History tells us that the Rashtrakutas served as vassals to the Chalukyas before they took over as rulers. According to legend, various dramatic events led to this. One version of the story is a bit like a fairy tale, and it goes something like this.

There was a king called Indra from the Rashtrakuta dynasty. He ruled from Ellichpur, which is the area around today's Ellora. Those were times when the Deccan was dominated by another dynasty called the Chalukyas. The less powerful dynasties like the Rashtrakutas were their vassals—which means that they probably had to pay homage to the

Chalukyas in some manner, like taxes or gifts or military support. In return, they were allowed to rule over a certain territory.

Indra was ambitious and wanted to expand his power. So, he decided to kidnap Bhavanaga, the daughter of the Chalukya king, Pulakeshi. He abducted the princess and later married her, hoping that Pulakeshi would concede parts of his kingdom to his son-in-law. But apparently, this ploy did not work because records show that the Rashtrakutas remained a vassal of the Chalukya kingdom.

This is probably an exaggerated version of a matrimonial alliance that was quite common among royal families of the time. It's more likely that Pulakeshi agreed to get his daughter married to Indra because he recognized that the Rashtrakutas had the potential to grow in power. But dramatic stories are always welcome, aren't they?

What happened after that?

Indra and Bhavanaga had a son called Dantidurga, who was a brave warrior. Indra died young, and Dantidurga became the king under the guardianship of his uncle Krishna. Dantidurga went on to become a favoured vassal of the Chalukya emperor, King Vikramaditya. Dantidurga fought many battles on Vikramaditya's behalf and helped him defeat Arab intruders and expanded the empire. After Vikramaditya died, Dantidurga continued to pay homage to the new Chalukyan emperor Keertivarman, but he was becoming too powerful for comfort. The Chalukyan king attacked the Rashtrakuta kingdom but was defeated, and with that Dantidurga became an independent emperor of the Rashtrakuta territory.

Five years after becoming emperor, Dantidurga died of ill health. His uncle, Krishna, became the emperor as Dantidurga had no son. Krishna continued to expand the borders of the Rashtrakuta empire by defeating the Chalukyas. Within a few years, the Rashtrakuta empire became one of the largest powers in the region, covering most of central India, Karnataka, Konkan and Andhra Pradesh.

It was during the reign of Krishna that the construction of the Kailash Temple at Ellora began. It went on to become one the greatest architectural monuments of India, still visited today by hundreds of tourists.

The Story of Buildings

Before we start exploring the awe-inspiring Kailash Temple, it would be good to understand what is architecture. Why is it important, and what has been the story of architecture in India since ancient times?

Architecture is the science of design of buildings such as houses, offices, places of worship and even things like bridges, airports and railway stations. In the past, people built shelters to protect themselves from the weather. The first houses were built with material that humans found around them—stone, wood or even leaves. As humans evolved, these shelters were clustered together in small communities. Staying close to others meant greater safety in numbers, and of course because humans are social animals—we like having neighbours! And that was how settlements like villages and towns began.

As human life became more complex, and it was not only about hunting and procuring food, humans started thinking of concepts beyond food gathering. Religion developed, and with it, rituals like prayer and sacrifice became common. This led to what is called 'religious architecture'—places where people could gather to worship. These were dedicated to gods and deities, and were built to symbolize the power of the gods. As time passed and humans acquired more and more knowledge of the natural world, and developed building techniques, the architecture of temples grew to be grand and elaborate. They were usually funded by royalty and built by the best craftsmen. At the same time, with society becoming classified into rich and poor, the powerful and the common, the king and the citizen, the buildings started reflecting these differences. Kings built palaces replete with rich materials and decorative elements that were brought from near and far, showing off their wealth and power through the architecture.

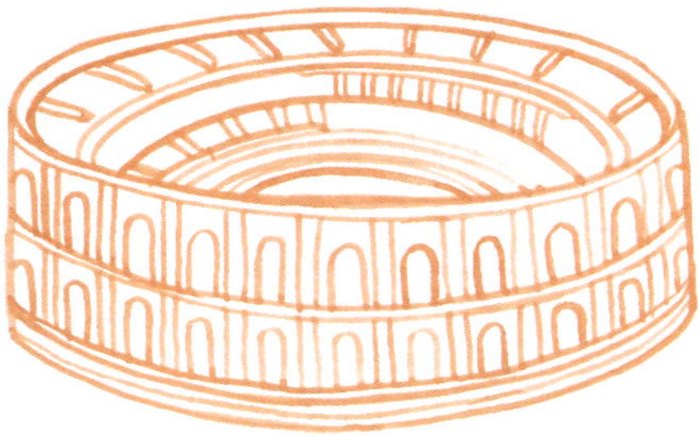

◆ Roman arena

◆ Pyramids

◆ Greek temple

Over several centuries, this developed into distinct architectural styles, often associated with a particular civilization or a dynasty. The ancient Egyptians built the great pyramids. The Greeks and the Romans developed what is now called classical architecture. India became known for its decorative carvings and embellishment in the structures. The Indian architects or master craftsmen looked at buildings more as sculptures than mere construction.

All Work, No Play?

To know the story of Indian architecture, we must take one more giant leap back in time. This time, to 4000 years ago to the Indus Valley Civilization. (Is all this skipping through time zones making you dizzy?) This civilization flourished in the Bronze Age (3300 to 1300 BCE). It was the earliest recorded settlement in the Indian subcontinent. Archaeologists have found traces of towns and cities along the Indus river at two major locations—Mohenjodaro in Sind and Harappa in southern Punjab.

In Harappa and Mohenjodaro, the cities were laid out along a grid. The houses were built of uniform-sized bricks, which was uncommon in other civilizations during that time. The remains of different types of buildings can be seen, like market-halls, stores, religious structures and public baths. There were extensive drainage systems. But curiously, while the Harappans seem to have used technology that would be considered advanced for the times, there were hardly any decorative or artistic elements in these buildings. The people of the Indus Valley seem to have been extremely business-like, practical and lacking an artistic touch. Or, the other possibility is that the society here was non-hierarchical, that is without distinctions of class. Maybe there were no kings and high priests in these societies and all citizens were equal. And therefore there was no need to make statements of power through the architecture. If it was the latter, then that would be quite unusual, wouldn't it? An ancient civilization that was free of class prejudices!

• *Layout of Mohenjodaro*

Over time, the Indus Valley Civilization collapsed. There are many theories on why this happened, including climate and geographical change, and constant attacks by nomadic tribes from the north-west. By the 2nd millennium BCE, the civilization had vanished and the cities of Harappa and Mohenjodaro emptied out.

◆ *Great Bath, Mohenjodaro*

Are-ya Planning to Live Here?

The next people who settled over much of north India are called the Aryans. They settled across the fertile Gangetic basin. They built small villages in the Gangetic plains instead of occupying the well-planned cities of the Indus Valley Civilization. What could be the reason for that? Maybe they preferred temporary settlements because they liked to keep moving? Have you heard of nomadic people who are constantly moving, usually with packs of animals which provide them their livelihood? There are a handful of such tribes still in the world who live a pastoral life, moving from place to place, like the Bedouins and the Gaddis. Maybe the Indo-Aryans were similarly dependent on animals and therefore moved around seasonally to pastoral areas.

The Aryans soon became an agricultural civilization and gave up their nomadic nature. Starting with simple hut dwellings, villages were formed around the agricultural fields. There are no architectural remains of this period but ancient scriptures like the Vedas and the Ramayana describe the dwellings of the time. These were mostly made of bamboo and thatch. Richer people used wood and clay tiles.

◆ *Types of Vedic dwellings*

With time, wood became the main material for construction. Vedic carpenters became highly skilled in timber technology. Most of the Vedic villages were built with timber, which is why none of these have survived.

• *Settlements were square in plan and streets were in a grid*

As the civilization developed, citadels and cities grew with protective walls and streets that divided the settlements into residential and commercial areas. Most often, these settlements were square in plan and the streets were perpendicular to each other, forming a grid.

Even though timber was used, a lot of construction with

stone began as well. Rock-cut caves and dwellings were created, and the technique used was similar to building with wood, even though stone as a material has very different properties.

Enter the Mauryans

One of the earliest dynasties of the Indian subcontinent was the Maurya. The Mauryans ruled over a large part of the subcontinent between 321 BCE and 185 BCE. They used a lot of stone in their buildings. A stone palace predating the Mauryan period has been discovered from the ruins in a place called Kausambi in Uttar Pradesh. The dressed stones of the palace were set in fine lime and coated with a thick layer of plaster and the entire architecture resembled a fortress with walls and towers.

In the 3rd century BCE began the reign of one of India's greatest emperors, Ashoka. His reign saw many changes in administration, religion, and the way rulers behaved with their subjects. Ashoka turned to Buddhism during his reign and thus started the Buddhist school of architecture during this time.

Many monasteries were designed for Buddhist monks. These were initially simple cave dwellings. Ashoka also built stupas and pillars. Stupas were hemispherical structures where the relics of the Buddha were stored.

Stupa is Sanskrit for 'heap'. Stupas were mounds with brick- or stone-facing that contained Buddhist relics. Ashes of the Buddha were buried in the early Buddhist stupas. Therefore, stupas went on to become symbols of Buddhist energy.

The Glorious Sanchi Stupa

The stupa at Sanchi is one of the oldest stupas in the world and a fantastic representation of early Indian art and architecture.

The Sanchi Stupa

Emperor Ashoka ordered it to be built in the 3rd century BCE. The location of the stupas was probably chosen by one of Ashoka's wives Mahadevi, who was a Buddhist and came from nearby Vidisha. The cluster of monuments at Sanchi, Madhya Pradesh, is now listed as a World Heritage Site.

In Sanchi, at the centre is a dome built of brick which contains Buddhist relics. It is crowned by a chhatra, or a parasol-like structure, intended to honour and protect the precious relics inside. The stupa is surrounded by four gateways called toranas that are carved with various scenes from the life of Lord Buddha and the Jataka tales. The national emblem of India was derived from the Ashoka Pillar that stands here.

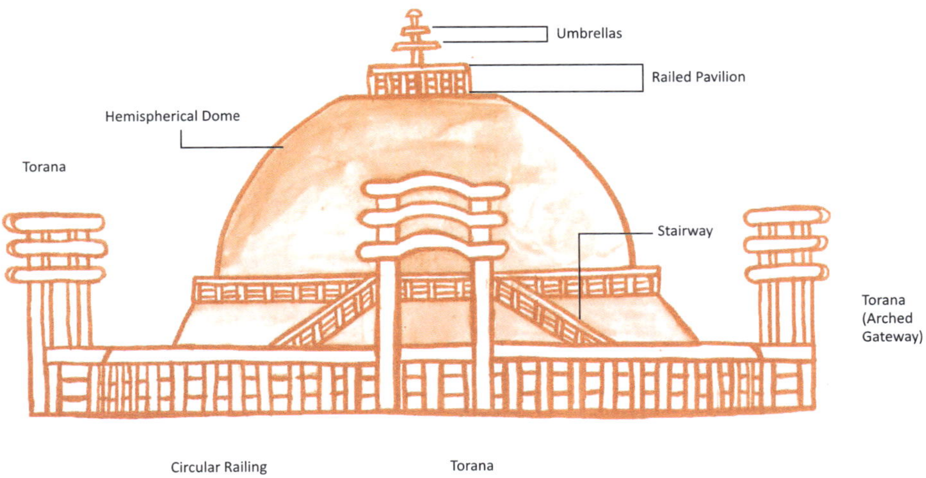

In 185 BCE, the Mauryan empire collapsed when the last of the Mauryan kings, Brihadratha, was assassinated by his general Pushyamitra Shunga who then took over the throne

and established the Shunga Empire. Many small kingdoms arose throughout India at that time. In the northern territories, a new empire arose when a ruler named Chandragupta I ascended the throne in 320 CE. His son Samudragupta extended the boundaries of the Gupta empire to cover large parts of northern India and even extending to the south.

During the long period dominated by the Guptas, there was a great flowering of art and architecture. The Guptas were patrons of art, literature, music, and this period has been described as the Golden Age of Indian history. But almost alongside the Guptas were some other great dynasties too—the Satavahanas and the Vakatakas are especially worth mentioning. The Satavahanas were great empire builders and they built the early Ajanta caves, not far from Ellora. The later caves at Ajanta were built in the 5th century CE by the Vakatakas.

The Caves above the River

The Ajanta caves were cut above the natural bed of a river. They are close to Aurangabad in Maharashtra. There are approximately thirty caves, with most being chaitya halls and viharas. Chaityas are prayer halls and viharas are monasteries where Buddhist monks live.

The earliest caves at Ajanta date from the 1st century BCE built under the patronage of the Satavahana kings, followed by the ones from the Vakataka period in 5th century CE. The Ajanta caves are known for the beautiful paintings on their walls. These are also called frescoes.

◆ *Frescoe at Ajanta caves*

During the Gupta period, Hindu temple architecture flourished. In Hindu religious rituals, the temple is a place where the devotee can be close to the deity. This led to the development of a sanctum sanctorum or the garbhagriha—the innermost and most sacred part of a temple where the deity was placed. The rest of the temple space revolved around this sacred room.

The temples were built using specific geometrical instructions that were laid out in the Vedas and ancient doctrines of buildings called the vastushastras. The plan of a temple was based on a square and the four cardinal directions, north, south, east, west. On top was the shikhara or a central spire that rose to a great height—this was to bring the deity closer to the heavens.

One of the few remaining brick temples from the Gupta period is at Bhitargaon, near Kanpur in Uttar Pradesh. It was built in the 5th century CE. It has a square plan which is topped by a brick spire or shikhara.

After the Guptas came the Rashtrakutas—the heroes of our story! By now Indian architecture was well developed. The Kailash Temple, which would go on to represent the peak of artistry of Indian architecture, would soon be built in the caves of Ellora.

◆ *Temple in Bhitargaon*

Those Magnificent Cave-men and -women

What comes to mind when you hear the terms 'cave-dweller' or 'caveman'? Do you think of men and women with long matted hair, dressed in animal skin making childish drawings on the walls of ancient caves?

Prehistoric humans started their settled lives in caves and similar natural structures. But as they evolved and started engaging in activities beyond hunting and gathering, caves became the canvas where early humans started expressing their imagination through art. Cave art was one of the earliest forms of artistic expression. The oldest known cave painting is a red hand-stencil in Spain. Scientists have dated this to 64,000 years ago—which makes its artist a Neanderthal man or woman! And the oldest drawing of an animal is of a bull, drawn in the caves of Sulawesi, in Indonesia, 40,000 years ago!

◆ *Ancient cave art*

These early drawings told the stories of the lives of those people and their times. While the term caveman is now used to describe someone who is 'wild' or the opposite of modern, cave-dwellers were actually evolved artists. This skill of excavating caves to make them places of shelter or sacred centres continued well into later periods and cave architecture became a sophisticated expression of a civilization.

◆ *Bhimbetka caves*

In India, too, this form of architecture developed thousands of years ago. Early rock art has been found in the **Bhimbetka** caves in Madhya Pradesh. These caves are an UNESCO-certified World Heritage site today.

Buddhism became an important religion during the Mauryan times and several early cave-temples were built by Buddhists. In later centuries, Hindu and Jain caves were built and the art of rock-cut caves reached its zenith around the 8th century CE.

Buddhist monks spent most of their lives wandering and preaching. The Buddha had said that monks should not stay in one location for more than a few days. But during the rainy season, it would be difficult for the monks to roam the countryside. The caves, traditionally, were places to shelter and rest for hermits in the Indian subcontinent. This is how the carving out of monasteries and prayer halls within the caves in the forests of India may have started.

The first cave excavations were in Bihar during the Mauryan era in the 3rd century BCE. Then cave architecture moved to western India and most of the rock-cut caves that have been discovered are located in the state of Maharashtra.

Rock, Paper...Wood?

Before we go on, let me tell you about a funny thing the early builders did. Today, when you see fancy homes you often see decorative tiles or stones placed over steel and cement structures to make the building look elegant. Guess what the ancient architects did to similarly make their creations look prettier?

During the Mauryan period, buildings were constructed mainly with timber. Indian artisans were extremely skilled in building large palaces and other structures using wood. Massive platforms, vaulted roofs, columns and foundations were all crafted skilfully by carpenters. When the trend of building rock-cut caves started, the artisans continued to use similar techniques in rock, and often replicated techniques that are used in timber construction, in stone. For example, a roof made of timber will need supports to prop it up, usually done by timber rafters or beams.

◆ *Timber frames*

A similar roof carved out in a cave will not need these supports. But ancient Indian architecture has examples where these types of supports were superficially added on.

In the early caves, we can see these details carved out even though they may not have been required because rock is far stronger and would not have needed the same treatment as timber. In fact, when archaeologists study these caves today, they find enormous holes carved in the rock surface that were possibly used to anchor wooden façades. Why did they do this? Probably to give it a 'modern' look. Over the centuries this trend disappeared as the artisans discovered how rock can be carved and treated.

◆ *A chaitya hall showing wood copycat structure*

But what was it that they were building? They were not simple homes to shelter in for a few days or months. The Mauryans and later builders were creating Buddhist prayer halls (chaityas) and monasteries (viharas) out of the caves.

Both of these followed certain common layouts. The chaitya hall consisted of a long hall with a semi-circular end. Architects call this an apsidal plan. This hall would be supported by two rows of columns, one on each side of a central prayer area called the nave. Next to the rows of columns, or colonnade, there was a side aisle. At the farther end of the long hall would be a stupa, carved out of rock. A stupa usually contained Buddhist relics, or remains and belongings of the Buddha and later prominent monks.

- *A section of a chaitya hall*

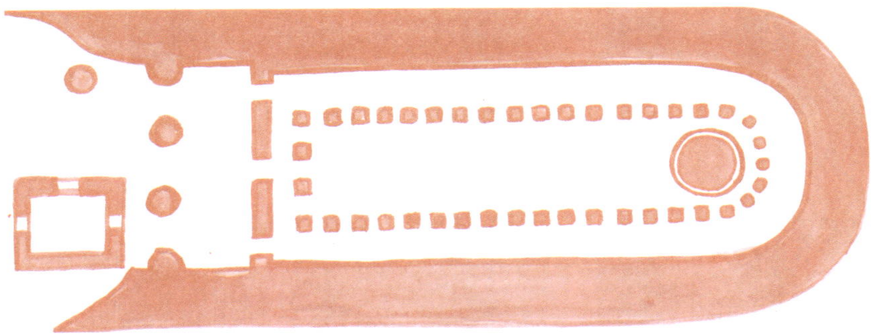

- *A plan of a chaitya hall*

Viharas had rectangular or square plans with cells or small rooms on the side and back walls. These were like small monasteries where Buddhist monks would reside, especially during the monsoon months. Later, the viharas also contained Buddhist icons sculpted in rock. These viharas became a combination of living quarters and prayer halls.

- *An elevation of a vihara*

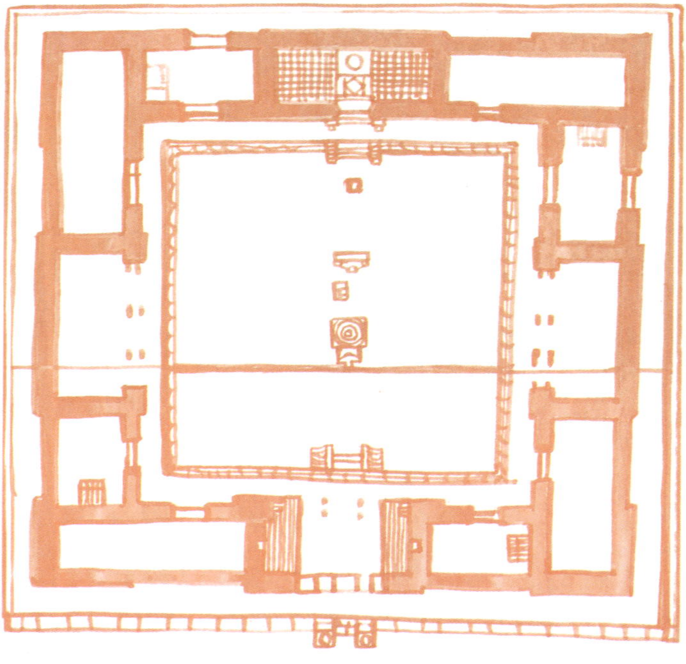

- *A plan of a vihara*

Kings Who Loved Caves

The rulers of the times loved cave-temples! Historians now know that royal patronage, or money, was poured into the development of cave-temples. As this form of art progressed, rich traders and royal families donated money, too, for creating grander versions of what started out as simple structures meant for monastic living. The later Buddhist caves in Ajanta have elaborate sculptures and frescoes created by extremely talented artists and craftsmen.

Buddhist caves can be dated up to the 7th century. After this, the religion declined in India. From around the 6th century CE, the Hindus started excavating rock-cut temples. Here, too, Hindu dynasties supported them. The earliest Hindu cave

- *Badami caves*

temples are found in Badami in the state of Karnataka. Built by the Chalukyan kings, the Badami caves have beautifully carved pillars, sculptures of gods and goddesses, intricate brackets and detailed ceilings carved out of rock.

A century later, the Pallava dynasty began the art of crafting monolithic rock-cut temples. Monolithic means these structures were carved out of single blocks of rock! Some early forms of this type of temples can be seen in the Pandava Rathas at Mahabalipuram in Tamil Nadu. They are five structures intricately carved to resemble chariots, each one created out of a single huge rock. As artisans became more and more skilled in using the medium of stone and rock, Hindu cave architecture became more intricate versions of the Buddhist caves.

◆ *The chariots at Mahabalipuram*

On the walls of these temples, scenes from the great Hindu epics like the Ramayana and the Mahabharata were carved out. Hindu cave architecture had common features too. There was a mandapa, or a columned hall in front of the sanctum space for the deity. The ratha—as seen in Mahabalipuram—is a chariot chiselled out of rock.

With the Kailash Temple in Ellora, rock-cut architecture reached its peak of skill and artistry. The temple was excavated out of colossal pieces of rock, and has all the features of a Hindu cave-temple, with chariots, pillars, mandapas and massive sculptures of gods and goddesses.

The third type of cave-temples that exist in India are the Jain caves. These developed between the 6th and 12th

◆ *A Buddhist cave-temple*

◆ *A Hindu cave-temple*

◆ *A Jain cave-temple*

century CE, in different parts of the country. Jain monks also roamed as mendicants and the natural shelter of caves was ideal for their frugal life. The Jain caves illustrate the tales of Tirthankaras who are worshipped by the sect. These caves were also elaborately carved and rich in sculptural features.

At Ellora, one can see the older Buddhist caves followed by the Hindu and Jain caves. The temple we are about to visit is the Kailash Temple at Ellora. It was a Hindu temple, built by the Rashtrakuta dynasty in the 8th century CE. It is the pinnacle of cave architecture in India.

The Man of Architecture

Before we start exploring Kailash, let us wander off to a side and hear the story of temple architecture in India. Don't worry, this too has interesting legends and myths associated with it.

The guiding principles of traditional Indian architecture is laid out in the Vastushastra. It dates back to the Vedic times, and was a basis for architects and their patrons to design buildings. It is a science based on mathematical calculations, traditional beliefs and natural phenomenon.

Vastushastra literally means 'science of architecture'. It's a set of traditional Indian principles that are used as guidelines for the design and planning of buildings. The system is based on Hindu and Buddhist beliefs and tries to integrate architecture with nature, geometric patterns and cardinal directions.

The first mention of Vastu was in the Yajurveda, which is an ancient Indian text, written almost 4000 years ago. According to its principles, Vastu Purusha is the presiding deity for all structures, whether they are temples or houses.

The foundation of Vastushastra is scientific. It combines the science of directions with the five elements—earth, fire, water, air and space—to create spaces that are best suited for certain types of activity. Imagine that you had to decide where, in a newly planned house, you would like your study to be. If you asked a Vastu expert, you would probably be advised to have the study table face north-east or east. While that may sound a bit random, there is a logic behind this advice. North-east and east are directions that receive morning light. Maybe studying in the fresh morning light allows better learning?

As with so many of our ancient texts, the Vastushastra also has an interesting legend associated with it. The story describes how the Vastu Purusha was created and then became the deity that seemed to give good advice on building design and construction.

Pin That Man, or, The Story of the Vastu Purusha

Lord Brahma created the universe and then he created the first man. This first man was no ordinary man. He was enormous in size and kept growing till his shadow covered the whole earth. The gods Shiva and Vishnu prayed to Brahma to stop this man from growing and destroying the earth. By then, Brahma was already regretting creating this all-consuming giant. But it was not going to be easy to stop him. Brahma could not do it alone. He asked the other gods for help. Forty-five gods, including Brahma, got together and grabbed the man and pinned him down to earth. Brahma jumped to the centre and held him down. The man's head was in the north-east direction and his feet pointed to the south-west.

Helpless and trapped, the man cried out, 'You created me. And now you have paralyzed me like this! Why?'

Brahma replied, 'You have become too destructive for the good of the universe. It's not your fault, but we need to stop you from destroying more of Creation.'

When he pleaded for mercy, Brahma said, 'I will make you immortal. You will be worshipped by all mortals who build any structure on the earth. You will be present in any land and you will be known as Vastu Purusha, the Man of Architecture.'

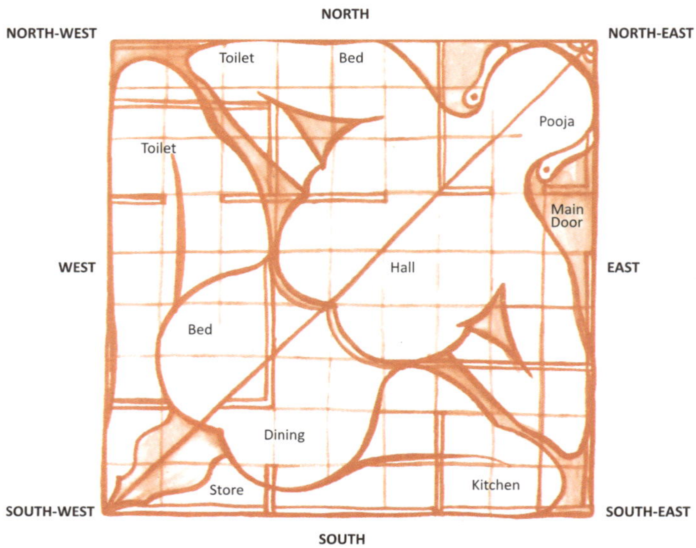

◆ *How the Vastu Purusha was pinned down*

Ever since, Vastu Purusha has been worshipped everywhere on earth. Every piece of land that's constructed upon becomes the Vastu Purusha Mandala. The mandala is an imaginary grid that divides the plot of land into sections. The pinned-down form of the Vastu Purusha is imagined to be contained within the grid with the head to the north-east and the legs to the south-west. It is a 9x9 grid made of eighty-one squares. Each square represents a god who pinned down the Vastu Purusha. There are forty-five gods in all, with Brahma occupying the central portion of the nine squares. Each of these gods must be kept happy while planning a structure. Vastushastra lays down rules on how to keep these deities happy. A house that is built keeping all the rules of this ancient text in mind promises to make its inhabitants prosperous and happy.

The Vastushastra spells out the location of rooms in a house. For example, the prayer room or living room or study room should be located on the north-eastern side of the house. This is because the sun is in this direction very early in the morning, which is the best time for prayer or studies or exercise.

The master bedroom of the house should be on the south-west side, because that's where the sun is in the late afternoon, a good time to rest.

Similarly, the Vastushastra advises the layout of all the rooms in a house, taking into account the position of the sun and the cardinal directions of the plot of land.

Where is your study or your bedroom located in your house? If it doesn't fall into the Vastushastra plan—do not fret!

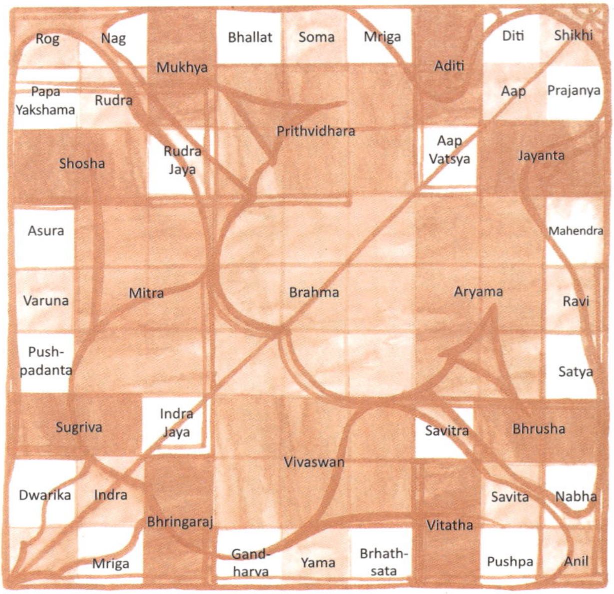

◆ *The Vastu Purusha Mandala with the eighty-one squares representing the forty-five gods who pinned down the Vastu Purusha*

These are just guidelines to help and many different factors contribute to being happy and successful.

Parts of a Hindu Temple

1. Garbhagriha

- Translated to 'womb-house' this is the main sanctum.
- In the earliest temples, it was a small square room at the centre of the main building, with a single entrance.
- The main deity is placed in this room and this is the most sacred part of the temple. Most rituals are held here and entry is often restricted to priests only.

2. Mandapa

- This is an entrance hall or foyer in front of the garbhagriha. It's usually a colonnaded space that allows a large number of people to gather. Devotees watch worship rituals from this area.
- Larger temples have multiple mandapas before you reach the sanctum—the ardha mandapa and mahamandapa are some of the names of these halls.

3. Shikhara or Vimana

- The shikhara is the tall spire of the temple which usually rises above the garbhagriha.
- The spire is called the shikhara in north Indian temples and vimana in south Indian temples. The shape of the spire varies from region to region.

4. Antarala (vestibule)

- The Antarala is a transition area between the garbhagriha and the mandapa.

5. Kalasha

- The pinnacle or the top-most point o the shikhara is called the kalasha.

6. Pradakshina Path

- This is a passage that wraps around the main sanctum area of the temple in a circular route. Devotees can walk around the sacred centre where the deity is kept. This action of walking around a holy spot is called pradakshina.

1: Garbhagriha, 2: Mandapa, 3: Antarala, 4: Pradakshina

◆ *Parts of a Hindu temple*

The layout of a typical Hindu temple reflects the Vastu Purusha Mandala as well. Different areas of the temple signify the location of the Purusha or Man. Here is how each part of the temple is equated with a part of the human body.

The garbhagriha (main sanctum) is the head; antarala (vestibule) is the neck; the ardha mandapam (half hall) is the chest; maha mandapam (main hall) is the stomach; gopuram or the temple gateway is representative of the feet. Most often the temple plan sits on a square grid of sixty-four squares in a

8x8 layout. The grid is like a framework on which the plan of a temple is laid out.

As we will see later, the Kailash Temple at Ellora followed this layout as well. The temple follows the main tenets of Vastushastra and is an example of a perfectly designed structure that keeps the Vastu Purusha happy!

What else does the Vastushastra say about designing temples? Here are some important Vastu tips for temples:

- The main shrine of a temple and the entrance gate should face the east as the sun rises from the east.
- The ideal direction for a temple to face is north-east.
- On entering the temple, the idols of the deities should not be visible to the devotees.
- Windows should be only on the eastern side.

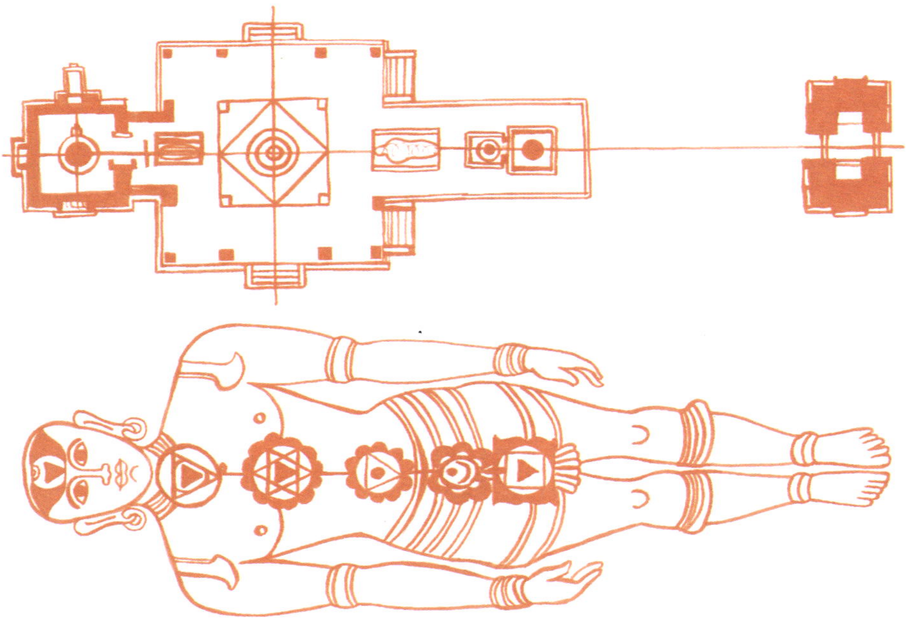

- *How a Hindu temple corresponds with the vastu purusha*

- Shoe-stands should be placed on the southern side of the temple.
- Water resources should be on the eastern side of the temple.
- The kitchen should be in the south-east corner of the temple.
- The sun rays should fall on the idols directly between 6 a.m. and 9 a.m.
- Devotees should have enough space to do the pradakshina around the idols.

There are several more which describe minute details of a temple layout. The next time you visit a temple, try and figure out the directions on a compass. Is it following these basic rules? In which direction is the main entrance of the temple? Is there a pradakshina path that you can walk on?

It would be fun to identify the main parts of the temple

too. Is the spire of the temple pyramidical or curved? Count the number of mandapas that lead up to the main sanctum. If the temple has a pradakshina path, walk on it and see where it takes you. You may come across smaller shrines dedicated to other deities scattered around the main shrine.

Temples in India are interesting places to visit. Their layout tells the story of our architecture and art. The deities that they house are part of our ancient mythology and scriptures. Each deity has many associated stories and fables around him or her. The rituals that are carried out in a temple have been followed for thousands of years and are part of our heritage as an ancient civilization. And temples are definitely places where you can watch interesting people come and go. They are usually thronging with crowds of pilgrims old and young, families and ascetics, flower sellers and confectioners, all making for an interesting mixture of sight, sound, smell, touch and taste!

Who Built the Kailash Temple?

Let us now enter the Ellora cave complex. Also called Cave 16, the Kailash Temple is a breathtaking sight as you approach it from the gates of the complex. Set against a cliff, Cave 16 looks like a gigantic painting. A sheer rock face of dark basalt spans the width of the entrance to the cave. The deep green of the trees, fresh from the monsoon showers, frame the entrance gate. Tall, carved figures guard the narrow passage below the grand arch of the gate and one can easily imagine priests and pilgrims walking into this cave with prayer on their minds.

When I visited the temple, as I walked towards it from the main entrance, several questions crowded my mind. Who was the person who built this magnificent temple? Who had thought about cutting through a massive rocky hillside with hundreds of masons and sculptors in order to carve out a perfectly designed temple? Who came up with the beautiful

◆ *The main entrance of Cave 16*

sculptures and friezes that would astound generations of visitors like us?

In the centuries past, the building of a temple required three types of people to be involved. There was the donor, or the **yajaman**, who was usually a rich person like a king or a landlord. He would have thought of building the temple, provided the land and also the money to build it. The **sthapaka**, or the priest, would plan the temple's spiritual character—the deities, how worship was to be conducted and such details. The third person was the **sthapati**, or the architect, who was responsible for designing the temple and then overseeing how it was built.

The Kailash Temple was built with the support of King Krishna I of the Rashtrakuta empire. He was the monarch of the empire from 757 to 772 CE. How do we know this? Because historians found an ancient copper plate while excavating the foundation of a house in Vadodara, Gujarat, and this information was inscribed on it. It's most likely that the idea of building such a grand temple was the king's idea. He would have also provided the funds to support the expenses during the construction. But it is impossible for an untrained person to design a structure that is as skillfully and almost perfectly planned as the Kailash Temple. That would have been done most certainly by a sthapati or an architect. Sadly, the name of this person is unknown. Perhaps there was a team of sthapatis who planned different aspects of the temple, and a team of master craftsmen—sculptors and masons—who worked alongside.

As with all ancient history, here again, there is a legend that describes how Kailash may have been built. According to this story, the king suffered from a severe disease. His queen prayed to the god Ghrishneshwar (another name for Shiva) at Elapura (now Ellora) to cure her husband. She vowed to construct a temple if her wish was granted and promised to observe a fast until she could see the shikhara (top) of this temple. After the king was cured, she requested him to build a temple immediately, but multiple architects declared that it would take months to build a temple complete with a shikhara.

One architect named Kokasa assured the king that the

queen would be able to see the shikhara of the temple within a week's time. He started building the temple from the top, by carving a rock. He was able to finish the shikhara within a week's time, enabling the queen to give up her fast.

Some historians say that Kokasa was indeed the chief architect of the Kailash Temple. There are mentions in some inscriptions from the 11th to the 13th centuries of architects born in the illustrious family of Kokasa. So maybe there is an element of truth in that story.

Let's Plan a Plan

Today, we study at schools of architecture or go to art school to train to become architects and artists. At these schools, we train for four or five years after which we are granted a certificate called a degree that allows us to practice architecture.

Landowners employ architects to help them design and oversee the construction of their buildings and townships.

In ancient India, the sthapati would study the traditional sciences called the Shastras. The Puranas, which were ancient collections of myths, were studied along with mathematics, painting and sculpture. It was also prescribed that a sthapati should be 'joyous, truth speaking, concentrated in mind, free from greed, carelessness and disease'. Most of us would possibly fall short to qualify to become a sthapati if we were tested on each of these! The knowledge that a sthapati gained was passed on to his sons or disciples. (Were there any women who studied this art? There are no records. But in contemporary times, there are as many women architects as men, so that's a good thing!)

If the sthapati who began a project could not complete it, the trained sons or disciples would be given the responsibility. It is entirely possible that Cave 16 at Ellora would have been built by more than one sthapati, because it took over a century to build the temple!

Imagine taking a hundred years to make one structure. Yet, the entire complex has a unified plan that looks like the design of a single individual. How do you think that was possible? In all probability, the original sthapati and his team passed on the work to his disciples who carried on the work without deviating from the original design.

As you have read in the chapter on Vastushastra, every step in the creation of a Hindu temple is governed by rules.

◆ *Temple with rock-cut hill*

The king would have consulted his sthapak and sthapati to choose an auspicious site. In this case, they chose a rocky cliff. At a time determined by the priest, the rocky hillside in Ellora would have been purified with rituals and the chanting of sacred mantras. A holy fire would have been lit to cleanse the earth of spirits that may have occupied the area. The temple would then have been constructed according to the rules of the Vastushastra, within a square, with the inner sanctum or the garbhagriha at the core of the complex. All other parts of the complex would have been similarly designed—the proportions and measurements derived from the rules laid out in the Vastushastra.

The first stage of the work was cutting the hillside to create the passages where pilgrims could take the ritual walk around the temple (pradakshina path). Stone masons would have worked for several months to excavate the rock down to the base of the hill, leaving an island of rock in the middle. The next job would have been to start carving this central island in great detail, starting from the top, to form the main Kailash Temple.

• *The excavation of Kailash*

The sthapati of Kailash Temple must have been a person with a fantastic imagination. He was able to visualize how the temple complex would be carved out of a rocky hill. From a single massive stone, he was able to design a three-dimensional structure that is considered an almost perfect form of temple architecture in India.

Drawing Inspiration

It is possible that the sthapati drew inspiration from some temples that had already been constructed by then. Some other such rock-cut temples are the Virupaksha Temple built by the Chalukyan kings in the town of Pattadakkal in Karnataka and the Kailasanatha Temple in Kanchipuram, built by the Pallavas.

It is no coincidence that temples using similar techniques are found in these places. The Chalukyans defeated the Pallavas and took over Kanchipuram. Later, the Rashtrakutas defeated the Chalukyans. In this transfer of power, the arts and crafts of the dynasties mingled and became even better. Maybe the craftsmen from Kanchipuram came to work on the temples at Pattadakkal, and when the Rashtrakutas started making the Kailash Temple, they used the same style as the Chalukyan craftsmen. **As each dynasty took over another, their arts and crafts came together** and styles of design kept evolving over the centuries.

If you look at the plans of the three temples, you will notice similarities. They obviously belong to the same family of temple architecture, like siblings from the same parents.

Both the temples—Kailash and Pattadakkal—have large gates or gopuram, a mandapa and a garbhagriha where the main deity is kept, encircled with a gallery for devotees to walk around the main shrine. Like the Kailasanatha Temple of Kanchipuram, Kailash at Ellora has smaller shrines around the path that circles the temple.

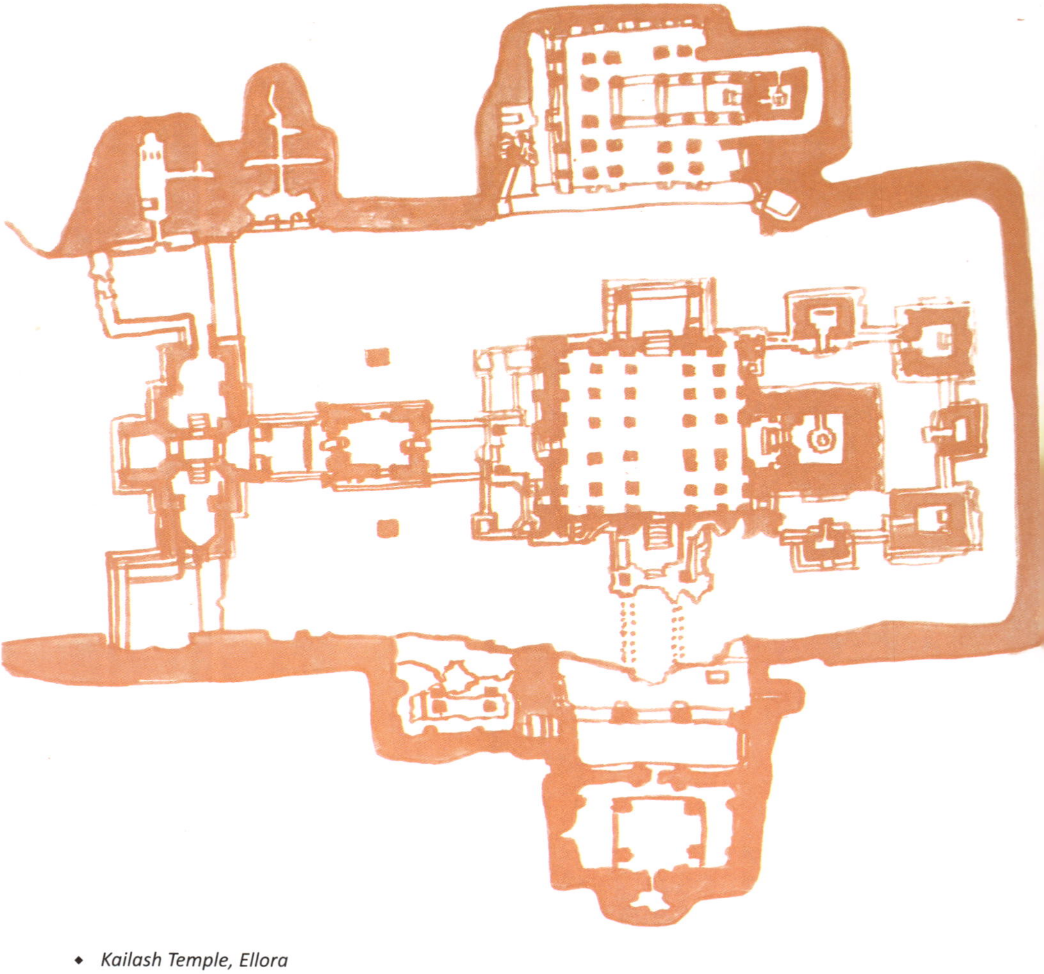

◆ *Kailash Temple, Ellora*

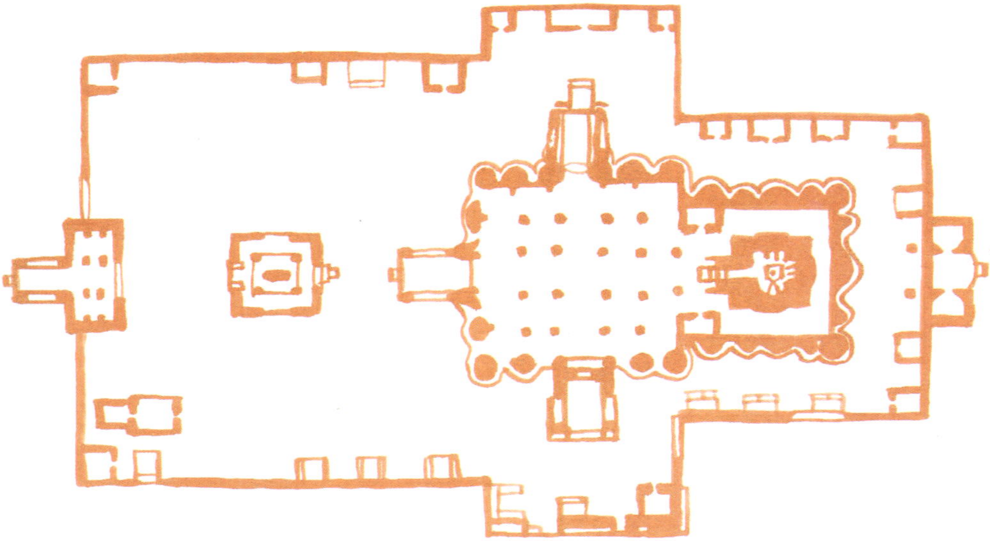

◆ *Virupaksha Temple, Pattadakkal*

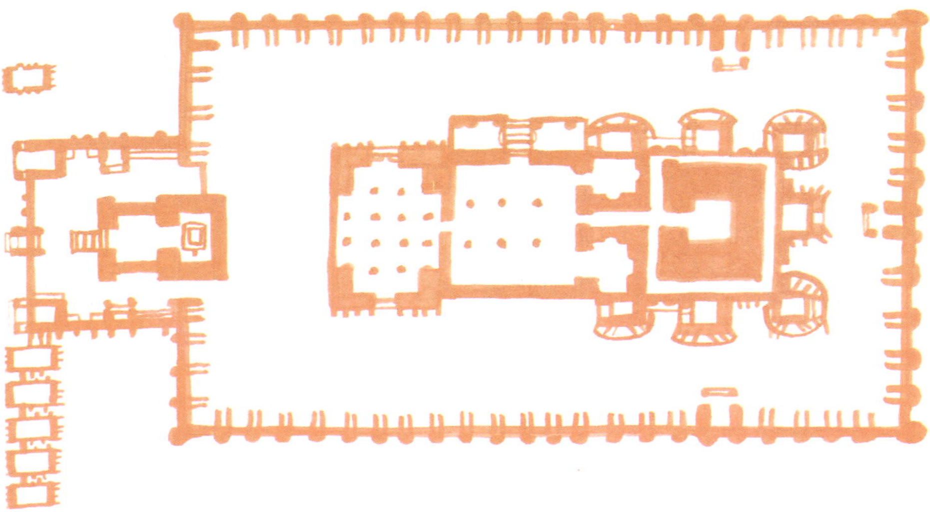

◆ *Kailasanatha Temple, Kanchipuram*

Working for 100 Years

It is estimated that 7000 craftsmen would have worked on the Kailash Temple for over 150 years. Yet, despite the passage of time and new generations of workers and designers, the temple has a clear design. Since it was made by cutting a single rock from top to bottom, each design and measurement would had to have been planned accurately, before construction began. Once it was cut, there would have been no chance to make corrections by adding pieces of rock or stone. Isn't that amazing, achieving such perfection without the technology of computers and drawing tools that are used by architects and engineers today!

How do you think it was done?

The sthapati of Kailash visualized how the temple would look, and may have made some rough drawings using measuring tools. He and his team were probably well versed in mathematics, so they could calculate measurements accurately to arrive at the plan of the main shrine which is a perfect square. They would have done such calculations by hand, hardly using any technology.

Today, architects and engineers use sophisticated software like CAD (Computer Aided Design) to convert their initial sketches into accurately measured drawings. These drawings are used by the team of builders to construct the building.

It is hard to imagine how the sthapati would have planned the sequence of work that involved cutting a solid rock face to create an entire temple complex. It probably took a lot of planning but there is no way to guess how this was done. Did the team of designers and site managers sit and write down a flow of activities which was then followed by site supervisors? We don't know. Today, in a large construction site, there is a project management team whose job is mainly to plan the flow of activities on the site. They see how they can complete the building in the minimum time, with minimum wastage of labour and money. These teams use softwares that help them to do the planning. Today, Project Management is an independent profession in the construction industry. I am sure these project managers could have learnt valuable lessons from the sthapati of Kailash Temple!

As you enter Kailash Temple, the scale of this project will become apparent to you. Come with me as I walk around the place, and we can imagine we are looking at groups of masons, sculptors and architects who are busy working there. Perhaps we can even join some of these teams and see how they went about their work!

Exploring the Kailash Temple

As we begin exploring this mighty and awe-inspiring temple, let us first pause and hear a story.

Stop It, Ravana, or, the Story of the Shaking of the Kailash Mountain

Ravana, the mighty king of Lanka, was a great warrior and a disciple of Shiva. He was an imposing figure with ten heads and twenty arms. Innumerable penances had made him strong and arrogant. As he went around conquering lands, he defeated his half-brother Kubera, whose kingdom, Alaka, was in the Himalayas. He looted the city and stole the Pushpak Vimana, Kubera's flying chariot. As he was about to fly over Mount Kailash, which was Shiva's abode, he was stopped by Nandi, Shiva's attendant. Nandi, the bull, told Ravana that Shiva and his wife Parvati were enjoying the views from the mountaintop and the Pushpak flying over them would create a great disturbance. 'So could you please circumnavigate Kailash?' asked Nandi.

Ravana was furious. Years of arrogance bubbled forth and he shouted, 'Who is Shiva?' Confident of his strength, he tried to uproot Kailash and started shaking the mountain vigorously. Shiva and Parvati were sitting on the mountain, along with their entourage, and were surprised to find the mountain quaking violently. Parvati clung to Shiva in fear. But Shiva was nonchalant. He held Parvati in his arms and with his right toe he pinned down Ravana, bringing the shaking to a halt. Ravana cried out for mercy. Shiva took pity on him and released him. From then on, Ravana became a great devotee of Shiva.

Now, let's meet this Ravana.

At the base of the Kailash Temple, on a wall on the southern side, you will come across a huge sculpture in stone, 20 feet high, that depicts this legend. It is set within a plain stone frame and looks like a theatre stage. On this stage, the story of Ravana, Shiva and Parvati is being acted out by the sculpted figures. Soaring above this tableau is the vimana or the towering roof of the Kailash Temple. Why is the sculpture of Ravana tucked away in the dark recesses below the temple? The answer is clear—the Kailash Temple at Ellora represents Shiva's home, the great Mount Kailash. So Ravana has to sit below this mountain-home to shake it as he shouts with rage.

Elephant sculpture
River Goddess Co
Front wall
Dhwajastan
Gopuram
Nandi Pavilion

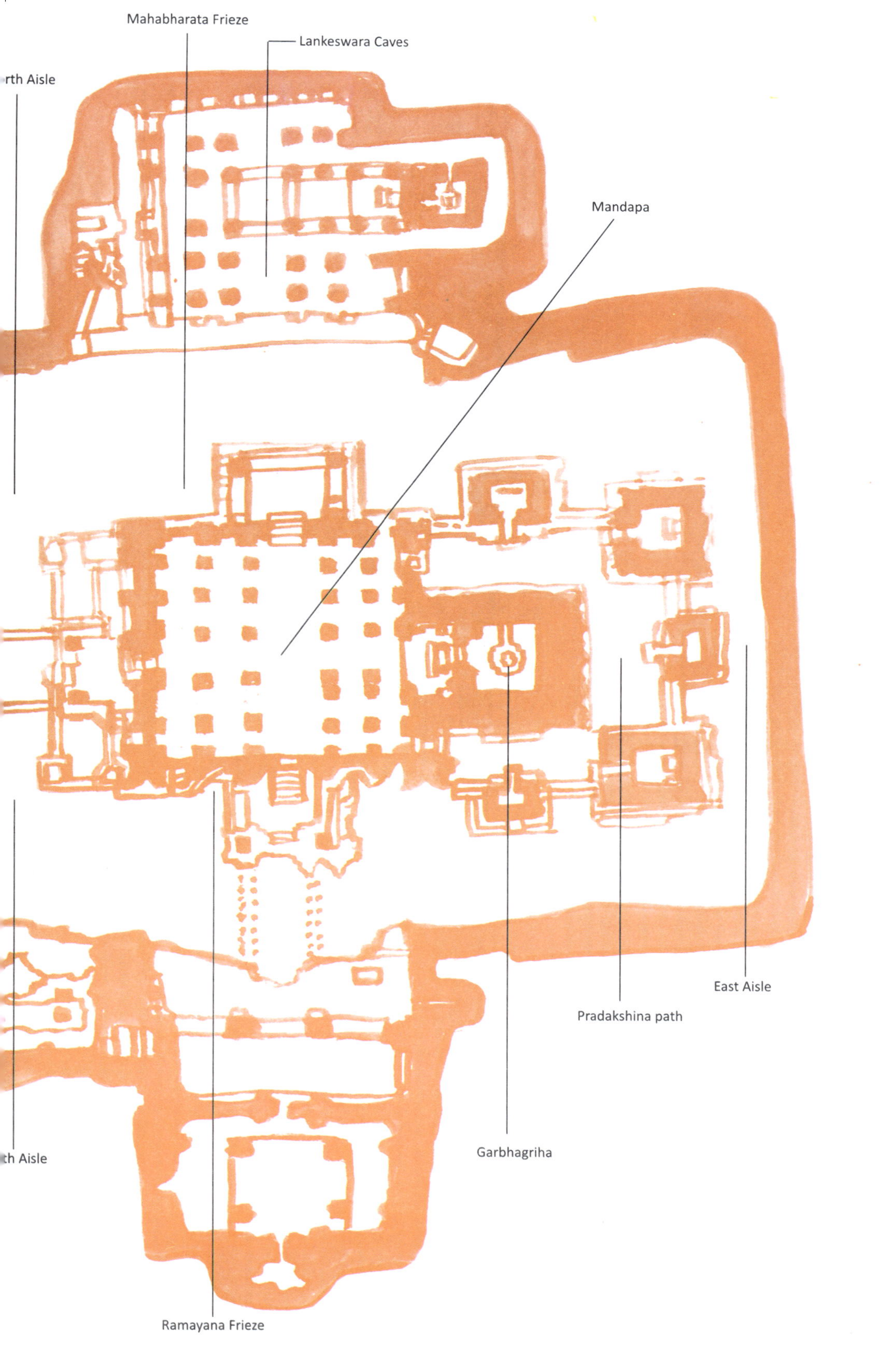

Mahabharata Frieze
Lankeswara Caves
rth Aisle
Mandapa
East Aisle
Pradakshina path
Garbhagriha
th Aisle
Ramayana Frieze

• *Ravana shaking Mount Kailash*

As we continue to walk around the temple complex, we will see how the Kailash Temple is an architect's representation of the mountain that is the seat of Shiva.

Did you know that there is a real **Mount Kailash** in the Himalayas? It lies in China and thousands of Hindu devotees travel to this mountain and trek around it as a pilgrimage to Shiva's home.

The Temple that was a Mountain

As we approach the entrance of Kailash, from a distance we can see a formidable wall carved out of the rocky ridge. Stretching about 150 feet across, the façade is flanked on either side by tall outcrops of natural rock face. At its centre is the main entrance tower which is called a gopuram. The gopuram is double-storeyed and carved out of rock. When we walk through it we see there are large sculptures on either

◆ *Sculptures at the entrance of Cave 16*

side, depicting various gods. Many of these have been partially destroyed over centuries of weathering and vandalism. Two interesting sculptures depict Agni, the god of fire, on his goat and Kartikeya, the god of war, astride his peacock.

At the end of the dark passage of the gopuram is a foyer that's open to sky and washed with natural light. Standing at this foyer, when you move your eyes from left to right, you will see the entire Kailash complex laid out before you. It is a dramatic moment—moving from darkness to light, from a narrow space into an open expanse. What do you think the architect wanted to show through this? Perhaps a pilgrim's walk from his earthly home to a space that belongs to a god—a god's abode? This is just one example of how built structures and architecture can create feelings of awe and devotion.

Architects often use such tools so that users experience things beyond what they see with their eyes only. This is

◆ *Gajalakshmi*

called artistic licence. In this case he was probably taking his visitor from 'darkness to light' because a place of worship is supposed to enlighten us.

At the foyer we are greeted by a large sculpture of Lakshmi, the goddess of wealth and prosperity. She is shown seated on lotus pads. Elephants hold up their protective trunks over her head from either side. This depiction of the goddess is called Gajalakshmi (Gaja means elephant in Sanskrit).

Now let's turn left to start our circumambulation of the complex. Hindus consider this circular walk around a holy space or deity as auspicious. It is called pradakshina and usually most temples have a path marked out that allows devotees to walk around the sacred area.

At Kailash, the main pradakshina path has been excavated out of the original rock. The temple and the central structures rise from the level of this path. Around the outer boundary of the complex there are various caves with sculptures. These form viewing galleries that look onto the path. They are also places from where you can view the temple from different angles. But remember, as you walk around this path and wander into the viewing galleries, every bit of construction here is actually an excavation. The gallery was once a rock face, as were the temple and the other structures. Out of one large rocky ridge, hundreds of sculptors and stone masons carved out this entire complex, using hammers and chisels.

When we turn left at the light-washed foyer, we step into a courtyard called the North Court. Facing the North Court is a

◆ *The River Goddess Complex*

rough-hewn cliff. At the base of the cliff is a beautifully carved cave called the River Goddess Complex. It's named so because the three sculptures inside this cave are believed to be the goddesses Ganga, Yamuna and Saraswati—three Himalayan rivers revered by Indians. Ganga stands in the middle on a makara or crocodile. On either side are her tributaries Yamuna and the mythical Saraswati. There is a depression in the cave floor that runs from one end of the cave to the other. Was this filled with water at one time? Possibly for visitors to perform a symbolic purifying wash like a dip in the Ganga? This could be another tool used by the architect to use design as a symbol!

The artisans of Kailash did not limit themselves to symbolic spaces to create this temple. Stories and legends cover the rock face in the form of carvings. These sculptures and friezes surround the visitor on every side. They depict stories about gods and mythical creatures from Hindu scriptures or folklore. Looking at these sculptures is almost like reading a comic book! In front of us are stories that have been depicted in three dimensions by ancient artists. Isn't that thrilling?

As we walk around, let's head closer to a few of these beautiful creations and understand the stories they are telling. After all, that is what the architects and artists wanted—that each visitor imbibe the stories of the gods. After seeing them depicted on the temple walls, people would carry back with them memories of what they saw and pass them on to their children. That is how ancient myths and legends have survived in many cultures across the world.

The Story of the Goddess Who Slayed the Buffalo-demon

In the North Court is a frieze carved on the wall that is called Mahishasuramardini, or Durga as Shakti, strong and heroic,

◆ *Mahishasuramardini*

protecting the people of the earth by getting rid of the evil asura.

If you look at the accompanying photograph, you will see a female figure with several arms, astride a lion. And near her feet is the slain demon, Mahishasura. The goddess is standing in a victorious pose and above her head there are smaller figures who seem to be looking down at the scene. These are the gods in heaven who are very relieved that the goddess has killed the demon who had been troubling them for ages. What is the story behind this frieze?

Mahishasura was a shape-shifting demon or asura who waged wars against the devas or the gods of Indralok. He wanted to rule the three worlds—Heaven, Earth and the Netherworld. After a prolonged penance, when Lord Brahma appeared before him to grant a boon, the asura asked that he should die only at the hands of a woman. Brahma agreed.

Mahishasura thought he was so strong and powerful, how could a mere woman ever defeat him. He thought he was now nearly immortal. Bad mistake!

He immediately unleashed terror on heaven and earth. His army of menacing demons started bullying and killing people on Earth and the devas in Indralok. Nobody could defeat him because of Brahma's boon. Fed up of his attacks, the devas appealed to the trinity of Brahma, Vishnu and Shiva to help them. Using all their powers, the Trinity created a woman, whom they named Durga. She had several arms, and in each

◆ *An idol at a Durga Puja*

hand she held a different weapon. Amongst these were Shiva's trident or trishula, Vishnu's flying wheel Sudarshana chakra and Indra's vajra or the thunderbolt. Durga, armed with her strength, power and wisdom, mounted a lion and set out to defeat Mahishasura.

When Mahishasura saw this powerful woman approaching him, his heart quivered. He remembered Brahma's boon that only a woman could kill him. He changed his shape into that of a buffalo and attacked Durga. After a fierce battle, Durga defeated Mahishasura. She became known as Mahishasuramardini, or the Goddess Who Slayed the Buffalo-Demon.

The slaying of Mahishasura is celebrated as Vijayadashami, a day of victory of good over evil.

Durga Puja is celebrated every autumn with great pomp in the states of West Bengal and Odisha. It is a celebration of the slaying of Mahishasura by Durga. Have you attended a Durga Puja celebration? For those few days, everyone wears new clothes and attends rituals at community celebrations. In Kolkata, the few days of the Durga Puja are like one continuous party with the whole city turning out on the streets, celebrating joyfully. The last day of Durga Puja is Vijayadashami, which also coincides with Dussehra.

Look right from the North Court, and there are two striking sculptures. The first is a life-sized sculpture of an elephant. Severely damaged over time, the elephant is still grand in size. The elephant was a popular motif of the Rashtrakuta empire and was often placed at the entrance of temples. Next to it is a free-standing stone column, like an obelisk. Carved from rock, this column has detailed decorations. The elephant and the obelisk form a screen between this area and the corridor beyond. Not only that, they have a symmetrical pair at the opposite end at the South Court.

From the North Court, we enter the dramatic North Aisle. It is a corridor designed to strike awe in the eyes of the visitor. On the left, there is a gigantic mass of raw rock that is projecting out on to the corridor. To the right is the beautifully carved spire of the temple. The space between these

◆ *North Court*

◆ *North Court and the North Aisle*

two is long and narrow with the sky visible above. Because of the proportions of this space, you will feel dwarfed. This is a result of the scale of the place. Architects often use scale to convey a feeling of power from the built structure. When you stand in the North Aisle with massive natural stone hanging over your head, you can feel the power of nature. Combined with the presence of the temple, it seems as though nature and god are overwhelming us.

- *A skyscraper*

Have you visited any famous place or monument that made you feel tiny in size? Like when looking up at a tall skyscraper in New York or while standing in the aisle of a huge cathedral? If yes, it's a result of scale. The designer of the building meant for you to feel tiny!

As we walk down the North Aisle, a flight of steps on our left takes us up to a gallery facing the path. These are the Lankeswara Caves. The corridor is dark and the walls are covered with sculptures carved on the rock walls. Several of these depict the god Shiva in various forms. Decorative columns line the external face of these caves. Let us stop a while and lean against one of these ancient columns and look out. You will be in for a surprise—for the view is simply breathtaking.

Deep below is the floor of the North Aisle. To the right you can see the elephant and the obelisk that we have just walked past. And in front of us, bathed in the daylight is the main temple. The temple's walls are carved with hundreds of scenes from the myths and Puranas. Entire stories can be read

- *The Lankeswara sculpture gallery*

on these walls. Look up and the huge stone temple will rise up like a giant emerging from the rocks. Pause a while and just watch the people walking around.

The sculptures that line the inner walls of the Lankeswara caves are dominated by Shiva doing various things—meditating, Shiva-Parvati's wedding and the most dynamic of all, dancing the tandava. Shiva breaks into a dance for different reasons, but he is best known for dancing the tandava.

Shiva's Tandava: The Divine Dance of Shiva

The tandava is a divine dance that is both violent and graceful. When Shiva is provoked, he does the tandava to express his anger and power. Here is a story that describes Shiva's tandava and its destructive power.

Brahma's son Daksha had a beautiful daughter named Sati. She was in love with Shiva and wanted to marry him. But Daksha would not allow this. He said Shiva was a wastrel spending his time in cremation grounds, covered in ash, accompanied by dogs and ghosts. But Sati and Shiva went ahead and got married. Daksha was enraged at this and refused to speak to his daughter and son-in-law.

Sometime later, Daksha arranged for a yajna, or fire sacrifice, and invited all the gods except Shiva. When she got to know this, Sati was very upset and went to confront her father. Daksha, however, refused to listen to her and instead insulted Shiva in front of everyone, mocking his son-in-law. Angered and in sorrow, Sati jumped into the ceremonial fire, killing herself. When he came to know what had happened to his beloved Sati, Shiva went mad with rage and sorrow. He started performing his dance of destruction—the tandava—while carrying Sati's charred body in his arms. He was so angry he wanted to destroy the universe to avenge Sati's death. As he danced, parts of Sati's body fell to the earth. The places where these parts landed went on to become sacred sites. There are

Shiva performing the tandava

fifty-one such pilgrimage spots or shakti peethas, scattered all over the Indian subcontinent.

Shiva's tandava was so terrifying that both mortals and the gods were afraid that the universe would end. Finally, Lord Brahma appeared and requested Shiva to forgive Daksha and stop his dance of destruction.

The tandava lives on even today! It is performed in different classical dance forms of India like Bharatnatyam. In this, the dancers perform energetic hand and feet movements to the chants of Shiva stotrams which are Sanskrit verses set to a tune and rhythm.

The sculptors of Kailash Temple have depicted Shiva's dance, and have infused a sense of movement even though it is carved in stone!

When we reach the end of the Lankeswara Caves we have to turn right. This is the East Aisle. From here, we will see a row of elephants standing with military precision at the base of the main temple. They look like they are holding up the entire temple on their mighty backs. Some of these elephants can be seen fighting lions and mythical dragons. Each of them is nearly life-sized and carved out of the natural rock.

Many of these carved animals are now damaged and broken but one can still feel the strength that the sculptor depicted by creating this line of elephants.

Try to imagine what the place would have looked like when it was under construction. In the beginning there was only a rocky outcrop. When the work started, the architect

and his team of stone carvers and sculptors would have stood on top of the rock and possibly marked out on the ground the plan as visualized by them. Then a large team of carvers would have set about with their hammers and chisels to slowly excavate the rock. The main temple and the adjoining Nandi Pavilion would have been carved from the top down. The shikhara would have been carved out right at the start, and the carvers would have slowly made their way down as they gave shape to the main walls of the temple. The pradakshina path would have required tons of stone to be excavated and removed from the site. Without engineering tools and machinery, how

Rows of elephants

do you think this was achieved? Maybe they used elephants to carry away rocks and rubble, as the complex slowly took shape? Did those elephants provide inspiration to the sculptors for the stone replicas?

But now, let us continue our pradakshina. When we stand at the eastern aisle, yet again there is an awe-inspiring sight. There is a giant chunk of solid rock projecting out from the gallery towards the centre of the aisle. This weighs 35 million pounds, and that is 30 feet of unsupported stone right above our heads! Can you imagine what would happen if erosion caused this rock to weaken? It would all come crashing down! This kind of projection of a building element that is supported only at one end is called a cantilever.

◆ *Stone cantilever in the East Aisle*

What is a **cantilever**? Imagine a plank of wood or a steel ruler. If you held this down at the edge of a table with something heavy and left the other end of it free, projecting out of the table, it would be a cantilever. Cantilevers are often used in constructing bridges where a large span needs to be covered without support. A fixed column at one end of the bridge provides the support and allows the horizontal span of the bridge to cover a distance over water or a mountain pass.

From the southern side of the path one can see the temple rising up to the sky. On the wall of the temple there are large sculptures that depict Sita's abduction by Ravana as the mighty Jatayu fought valiantly to stop him. There's Vishnu in his avatar of Narasimha—half-man, half-lion—slaying the evil king Hiranyakashyapu. These episodes and stories are depicted in such detail that they look like the figures are leaping out of the stone.

The Abduction of Sita

The abduction of Sita is a dramatic episode in the Ramayana. Ravana, the king of Lanka, was furious with Ram and Lakshman for insulting his sister Surpanakha by chopping off

◆ *The abduction of Sita*

her ears and nose. This violent encounter between the two princes and the demoness happened in the forest where Ram, Sita and Lakshman were spending a fourteen-year exile.

Ravana decided to abduct Sita and avenge his sister's insult. After luring away Ram and Lakshman from their forest cottage, Ravana disguised himself as a mendicant hermit. He appeared at Sita's doorstep, begging for alms. When Sita stepped out to give him an offering of fruits, he grabbed her by her hair. Magically transforming himself back into his ten-headed form, he dragged Sita to his chariot and flew off towards Lanka. As his chariot sped away, he was stopped by the valiant bird Jatayu, who tried hard to save Sita by attacking Ravana. But Ravana was far stronger than Jatayu. Leaving the bird injured, Ravana flew across the ocean and reached his kingdom of Lanka. Sita was kept captive in the Ashokvana, guarded by terrible looking demons, till Ram, Lakshman and their army of monkeys came and rescued her after killing Ravana.

The Ramayana is one of the oldest epics in the world, with some estimates dating it back to the 8th century BCE. It was originally written in Sanskrit by Maharishi Valmiki, or so the legend goes. The story traces the life of Ram, a prince, who is sent to exile with his wife Sita and his brother Lakshman. The Ramayana ends with the prince returning to his kingdom Ayodhya, after rescuing Sita and defeating Ravana. The return of Ram to Ayodhya is celebrated as Dussehra, which is a day of celebration all over India.

Have you seen Dussehra festivities? Large effigies representing the ten-headed Ravana are constructed and filled with firecrackers. Actors dressed up as Ram, Lakshman and Sita enact scenes from the Ramayana in front of adoring crowds after which Ram shoots flaming arrows at the effigy which bursts into a display of fireworks, marking the victory of good over evil.

The Story of How Hiranyakashyapu Was Defeated

Hiranyakashyapu was an asura and king of the daityas (a clan of asuras). His brother had been killed by Vishnu, in his avatar as a boar, or varaha. To avenge his brother's death, Hiranyakashyapu did a long penance to gain mystical

◆ *A sculpture of Narasimha*

powers. At the end of many years of austerity and prayers, Lord Brahma appeared before him and granted him a boon. Hiranyakashyapu asked for immortality but Brahma said that was impossible. But the asura was adamant and after much calculation, he asked Lord Brahma to grant him a boon that would allow no man, god or animal created by Brahma to kill him. Also, nobody could kill him at day or night, and no one could kill him in heaven or on earth. He could not be killed with a weapon, or killed inside or outside his house.

With this boon, Hiranyakashyapu became victorious in every battle and banished the devas from Indralok. But by a quirk of fate, his son Prahlad was a gentle and spiritual boy and a devotee of Vishnu. This infuriated Hiranyakashyapu. He tried to change his son's mind but failed. Angered, he even tried to get Prahlad killed in various ways, but each time the boy got saved. It seemed like he was being protected by Vishnu himself.

One day, Hiranyakashyapu asked Prahlad if Vishnu was present in his room. When Prahlad replied that Vishnu was always there for him, Hiranyakashyapu flew into a rage and mocked him. He pointed at a pillar in the room and asked if Vishnu was in the pillar. When Prahlad said yes, he kicked the pillar in rage. The pillar cracked open and a ferocious creature —half man, half lion—came out. This was a form taken by Vishnu in an avatar called Narasimha.

This strange and fierce half-man and half-lion dragged Hiranyakashyapu to the threshold of the door, which was neither outside nor inside his house. He placed him on his lap, which was neither the sky nor the earth, and killed him with his claws at twilight, without using any weapons. Thus, all the conditions of the boon were fulfilled, and yet Hiranyakashyapu was destroyed. Prahlad was made the new king and Vishnu blessed him.

Carved on the wall of the main temple, the frieze shows the fierce expression on Narasimha's face as he kills the evil king.

As we come to the centre of the southern aisle, we see the

sculpture depicting Ravana shaking Mount Kailash. We started our walk around the complex with this story. Now that we have experienced the scale of the Kailash complex and seen how the architect thought of it as a representation of Mount Kailash, it makes sense that this theatrical sculpture of Ravana was located at the base of the temple, in a dark recess. It emphasizes the power of Lord Shiva, who, while seated on Kailash, subdued such a strong warrior by merely pressing down his right toe.

Symmetrical to the North Court, the pradakshina path ends in the South Court which has another life-sized elephant sculpture and a beautifully detailed free-standing column that mirror the one we have seen in the North Court.

From the South Court, a staircase leads up to the foyer of the main temple. Here, look carefully at the ceiling, and you will see paintings that are faded. More sculptures adorn the walls that face the foyer.

Before entering the main temple, we cross a bridge and

Symmetry is a powerful tool in architectural design. It gives a building a sense of balance and a definite start and end point. It also usually defines a central focus of a building around which other elements are arranged in a geometrical fashion. Symmetry has been used in architecture from ancient times. If you visit the Pantheon in Rome or the Taj Mahal or the Empire State Building in New York, you will see symmetrical designs.

- *Nandi, the bull*

enter the Nandi Pavilion. This is a square room with a statue of Nandi, the bull, in the centre. This statue was probably placed in later times. Walking further ahead, another bridge takes us to the first floor of the gopuram. A balcony at this level allows us to look down at the entrance of Kailash and the gardens that we had crossed when we walked into the complex.

The gopuram is exactly at the centre of the Kailash layout. From here, you can walk to the right or to the left onto open terraces on either side. Isn't it fascinating that the rock walls are so thick that they can be used as terraces? If you stand on either of these terraces, facing inwards, you will look back into the North and South Aisles and can see the temple complex from a higher level.

- *View from above the gopuram looking onto the pradakshina path*

The excavated pradakshina path can be seen from here. Visitors to the temple look dwarfed by the monolithic elephants and the obelisk-like columns. The shikhara of the main temple rises up towards the sky and standing on the terrace, you can see the intricately carved walls—full of stories that take people back to a time when legends seem to have ruled the earth. At the opposite end of the Kailash excavation, the sheer rock face of volcanic basalt is visible. It's fascinating to think that this rock would have been witness to hundreds of craftsmen working in the excavation pit, as the temple complex slowly evolved.

Walking back towards the temple, we now enter the main hall. Elegantly carved square columns support this hall, which is called the mandapa. It's dimly lit and devotees would gather

The main hall

◆ *The inner sanctum*

here to see the deity. The only light entering it is from the doors and the stone-grilled windows. On the ceiling there are more sculptures of Shiva and Parvati.

At the end of the hall are a few steps leading up to a small room that has the main deity of Kailash. The deity here is a stone that symbolizes Shiva—the Shiva lingam. This room is the most sacred part of the entire complex and is also called the garbhagriha. When the temple was used for rituals, devotees would have gathered to pour milk and ghee over the lingam and offered flowers and sweets along with prayers. Incense would have filled the air, and oil lamps would have flickered casting shadows on the walls. Today, visitors still remove their shoes at the door of the mandapa as a mark of respect to the sanctity of the space. But no rituals are performed here any longer.

◆ *Paintings on the ceiling*

Doors on either side of the mandapa lead us onto the final pradakshina path that takes us around the mandapa. As we walk along this, one by one we come across five smaller shrines with the main shikhara rising majestically in the centre. The raw cliff walls that border the Kailash complex which we saw during our walk in the lower pradakshina path, now seem close enough to touch. They form a dramatic backdrop to the decorative shikharas of the small shrines that we walk past.

Completing the circle around the vimana, we walk down the staircase that brings us to the North Court yet again. Now it's time to look closely at the outer walls of the temple. There are a series of carved panels here.

If you look closely, you will find that these panels depict stories from the Mahabharata. You can spot Arjuna sitting on

◆ *Mahabharata panel*

a chariot facing armies lined up for war, and Krishna speaking the words of the Bhagvad Gita. As everything is symmetrical at Kailash, the wall on the South Court has a similar series of panels showing the stories of the Ramayana. You can spend several minutes standing in front of these panels, trying to guess which incidents from these famous epics are being related on the panels.

Let's sit awhile here on a stone ledge at the entrance and soak in the details that occupy every corner of the Kailash Temple complex, Cave 16 at Ellora.

Visiting Kailash Temple Today

The walk around Kailash takes you back in time. Yet, we have to remember that it's a heritage that we have been gifted and that we need to protect.

While walking around the Ellora caves and the Kailash Temple, I have been struck by the thought that such a beautiful creation is almost impossible to be made by the hands of humans. The perfect geometry, the beautiful sculptures and carvings all set against the backdrop of the hills and greenery make the Ellora caves a true wonder of the world. One is tempted to believe legends that claim that extra-terrestrials with advanced technology flew in and built these amazing structures. (Yes, such theories do exist!) But the reality is that it was created several centuries ago by men and women, with ignited minds and hands that had the skills that cannot be matched by modern inventions.

When you visit the place, remember that behind the magnificence of these structures are individuals, just like you and me, doing a work of passion. Every mason, sculptor, painter or designer who put his mind into this creation had

a significant role to play. It was a team of people that carved down the Sahyadri hills and just like playing tag, passed on their designs and skills to next generations to complete the picture, without a stone looking like it was out of place.

A Lesson in Tolerance

The caves get thousands of visitors every year. Some people come to the caves because they are sacred sites. For others, it is the historical and artistic aspects that draw them here.

Besides the rich architecture and art, Ellora has another feature that makes it unique. In the pages of history, you will read how the dominant religion of a time and place displaced all other religions and their places of worship. Every dominant religion has a mission to convert more people into its folds, and historically, this has resulted in conflict, destruction of religious property, and a disturbance of communal peace. In Ellora, there are thirty-four caves belonging to three different religions—Buddhist, Hindu and Jain. And although they have been excavated over different periods of time, they have continued to co-exist. There has been no desecration of the caves of one religion by another. It's a space that respects and accepts all the sects that inhabit the space.

The Ellora caves therefore illustrate the tolerant spirit of India with sanctuaries of three different communities within its premises.

Don't you think such places are as valuable as our stock exchanges and industries and should be preserved for generations of people to come and marvel at these caves?

Preserving Ellora

While we are proud and lucky to have inherited such a rich architectural heritage, as a civilized society we need to know how to protect this inheritance. The Archaeological Survey of India (ASI) and UNESCO are organizations that have taken on this task and have been protecting these monuments. Ellora became a UNESCO World Heritage Monument in 1983. This allowed funds to be allocated for a variety of measures to be taken at all the caves within the complex. The Kailash Temple gets a major chunk of the ASI's attention as part of the ongoing work, since it is one of the largest and most visited excavations at Ellora.

While you are wandering in the caves, keep your eyes peeled to spot any damages or even signs of repair work that may be going on. You may notice scaffolding frames that have been erected to protect parts of the caves, or signs that warn of unstable rocks. If you are observant enough you may see ASI staff cleaning sections of sculptures and frescoes armed with brushes and other fine archaeological tools. These teams of conservators and engineers look at every inch of the caves, keeping their eyes open for any sign of disrepair.

You may be wondering what damages ail such ancient caves. The fact that these caves have survived almost 2000 years of existence is a wonder. Surely over all these centuries, local inhabitants and royal patronage must have actively participated in protecting these caves—a reason why they have not been completely eroded by natural and man-made action. In the last 200 years, with rapid increase in population and industrialization, the wear and tear that such places have faced is even more intense.

In modern times, the caves have been affected by pollution, excessive tourism and climate change. In addition to these, cave monuments have their own set of challenges. The unique micro-climate in caves allow microbes, algae, fungi and insects to flourish due to the low temperature, little or no sunlight and high humidity.

As you would have noticed, the caves are built into the hillside. Which means that they are also affected by the natural vegetation that grow on the hills. Trees growing above and along the caves push their root structures into the walls and roofs causing cracks and dislodging stone and rock. During the monsoons, water seeps in through these cracks which leads to damage to the wall paintings and the sculpture. Water seepage increases dampness causing an increase in algae, insects and microbes. If you are adventurous enough, maybe you could try and spot some insects too! ASI reports record beetles and silverfish to be commonplace.

Bats often infest caves, nesting in dark, humid corridors—their faeces is a common source of damage, besides the horrible smell that engulfs any space that these creatures inhabit. Did you know that the earliest fossils of bats date back to 52 million years? That makes it even more astounding—a prehistoric mammal still surv˙ves as a spec˙es and their descendants are currently making homes in man-made temples and terrifying people with their ghost y behaviour! So go ahead and spot a few before the ASI drives all the bats away.

And finally—tourists—who are often unscrupulous and vandalize and even steal from these caves. It's not unknown for ASI to discover that parts of sculptures are chiselled away and stolen. Walls of caves are defaced by graffiti and the presence of crowds often result in littering. Try and spot how frequently you encounter garbage bins. And if you see people littering or spitting, stop them. Young crusaders for the environment like you can make your voices heard well above posters, notices and fines that a government can put up. Environmental activist, Greta Thunberg, is a hero who started a campaign as a single voice that grew to a worldwide movement. Get inspired and be an inspiration.

How to Conserve Heritage

How does a conservation body carry out its responsibility? At Ellora, ASI takes various precautionary measures to protect the premises. All cracks and structural instabilities are addressed by adding supports. Water seepage is prevented by creating rainwater drainage systems and waterproofing layers are added where it's possible. Insecticides and herbicides are sprayed. Some portions of the Kailash Temple have been enclosed with wire mesh to prevent bats from nesting. Conservation efforts include regular cleaning, adding a preservative coating on paintings and fixing loose plaster on the walls. A mixture of hemp, clay and lime plaster is used to preserve the paintings and carvings. Security guards patrol the caves and keep an eye on potential miscreants. Stringent security checks ensure that people are unable to carry tools that allow them to mischievously break away a head and carry it away in a handbag! Only certified guides are allowed to show tourists around and narrate the stories and history. And if you are handicapped, there are wheelchairs on hire and ramps constructed in places that allow everybody to see all major areas of interest.

A Helping Hand

Here is an interesting personal anecdote. One of my visits to Ellora was nearly cancelled because I fractured my foot, while in Delhi. Determined to go ahead with the trip, I flew to Aurangabad and landed at the ticket counter at Ellora, hobbling on crutches. I was a bit nervous since I knew that the terrain at Ellora was not easy for anyone with a physical disability. And was I glad that I had allowed myself to take a chance! There was a row of wheelchairs to choose from and I was told that I could hire a guide who would also help push my wheelchair around the premises. I was delighted when Mr Sanjay, the guide, not only trundled me back and forth the rocky roads of Ellora while describing the caves, he also helped me walk up and down steps where there were no ramps! My research would have been incomplete without this experience.

Mr Sanjay was a great source of interesting stories that abound in Kailash. Have you ever followed a guide down the corridors of a palace or stood in a historical precinct in a strange country and heard stories of battles fought and kingdoms lost? When I visit a place of history, I always hire a local guide. There are two reasons for this. One is the obvious—listen to the local myths along with the recorded history. If you delve deeper into the guide's narrative and ask questions, the fables and myths will come tumbling out. These are often more interesting than what you read in books, even though they maybe fictitious or concocted. A bit of imagination will only make you see a place of history with greater richness.

- *Sanjay and me*

The second reason that I have for hiring a guide is to help the local economy. Most tourist attractions support the population by creating opportunities of income. The guide, the postcard-seller, the boy selling key chains or even the coconut-seller outside the entrance earn daily wages from tourists. If you can afford one or more of their services, do not hesitate to buy. You would be helping local families earn a dignified income. And maybe you will make a friend in the process.

On an earlier visit to Kailash, I was standing in the mandapa of the Kailash Temple, my two daughters in tow, trying to squint in the darkness and figure my way up to the inner sanctum. Suddenly, a figure appeared next to me. A genial man in a dhoti, with eyes that sparkled in the dark, he switched on a torch and announced, 'Are you lost? Let me show you around.' Waving his torch around he said, 'Mind you, I am not a guide. I clean the temple. I spend the whole day here and you won't find a better person to show you around.' We followed his torch as he pointed at the ceiling and at the walls, showing us frescoes and carved pillars that would have gone unnoticed otherwise. In an animated voice, he described myths about the Goddess Durga, making us peer at some painted figures in the dingy corners. As he led us into the garbhagriha where the Shiva lingam is kept, he said, 'This is the holiest part of Kailash. You can pray to the god here and make any offerings.' And with those words, he disappeared into the darkness again, like the genie of the lamp, carrying away his torch that had been throwing light for the last twenty minutes. I did not see the gentleman again, nor did I pay him anything for being a temporary guide to us. But we figured that there is a larger ecosystem of people who live in the shadow of the Kailash Temple, who see this place as home. Enjoy such encounters, because they bring the place alive—from a tourist spot to a building that wakes up every morning with its inhabitants and plunges into darkness every night as lights are switched off.

The Importance of Time Machines

While conservation societies protect our monuments and ensure that their physical well-being is taken care of, it's important that we create environments that allow curious visitors like you and me to understand the time in history when a monument stood. Who built it? What inspired the design? How was this space used when it was first built? Did it bustle with people? Did children play in corners and did animals roam in the forests nearby? Were there craftsmen selling knick-knacks at the gate, like the postcard-seller does today? Was there the fragrance of incense and the sounds of mantras being chanted as the priests performed daily rituals at the temple sanctum?

Wouldn't it be interesting to be transported back in time, like in a time machine? Maybe future conservation efforts will include new technology to allow us to experience such realistic recreations of times gone by.

What would you like **to see from the past** when you walk into a cave at Ellora? Write and describe a few things on your wishlist.

Our journey into ancient Indian architecture and its evolution to its zenith with the Kailash Temple took us through different stages of Indian history. Which bits interested you the most? Was it the Harappan people with their precise and practical settlements? Or did the legend of the vastu purusha intrigue you enough to find out which direction your front door opens to? Whichever nugget of information fired the neurons of your brain, do dig deep and find out more. Knowledge is as rich as the sculptures of Kailash. As you brush away the clutter around information and myths, like an archaeologist cleaning the dust around a fossil, a story will emerge that will leave a mark in your mind forever.

Author's Note

Have you wondered how these fantastic monuments are built so perfectly—symmetrical, every side of the building meeting at perfect corners, not a window out of place? That is because most buildings start as drawings on paper (and now on the computer using design software).

There are three basic drawings that architects make to explain the design to the construction team. These are called Plan, Elevation and Section.

Together, they represent a building graphically. These drawings are two-dimensional representations of the building—as if the building was a flat object. In this way, a whole room or building can be shown on one piece of paper. To fit the whole building on paper, the drawing must be drawn to a scale. That means 1 centimetre on the paper might represent 100 centimetres in the real world.

A **plan** is a drawing of a building as seen from top—like a bird's eye view. Imagine taking the roof off a building and looking down inside it. What you see is what an architect calls the floor plan. It shows the layout of a building with all the dimensions marked out. It is the main drawing that is used when construction starts.

◆ *Plan*

◆ *Plan*

An **elevation** is a drawing of a building as seen from one side. It could be the front or side of the building. It gives the viewer an idea of some key features of the building such as height, length, width and external appearance. Architects use elevations to study the external appearance of a building.

◆ *Elevation*

Section drawings give a more complete idea of what a building might look like when it is built. They are drawn from a vertical plane slicing through a building, as if you sliced it from top to bottom and stood looking straight at it. It is used to show the heights and vertical measurements. These drawings allow us to see the features inside a building.

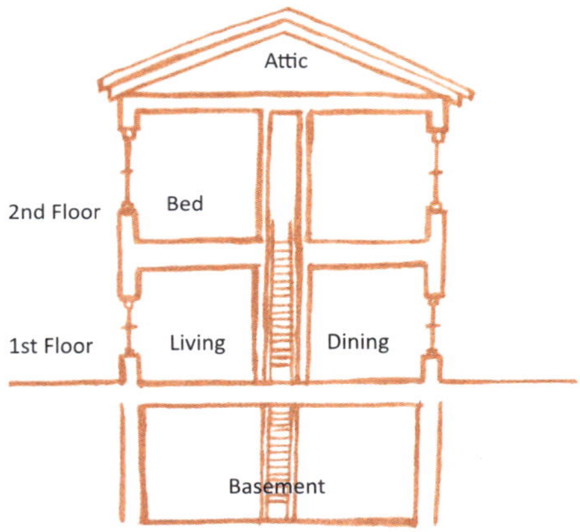

◆ *Section*

◆ *Section*

Acknowledgements

The reason I jumped enthusiastically into writing this book on the Kailash Temple at Ellora was so that I could engage in legitimate research and hence travel to the caves and snoop around. Satyajit Ray and the Feluda-Topshe-Lalmohan Ganguly trio have immortalized Ellora as a place of adventure in the Bengali detective story *Koilashey Kelenkari* and I was raring to find that for myself. I made a couple of trips, each of which stunned me with the beauty of the whole geographical location and specifically, Kailash with its epic beauty. Therefore, my first acknowledgement has to be towards Satyajit Ray and Feluda. Though Ellora seemed free of art-smugglers when I visited, the whole complex had the scent of a sleuth I have long admired and it was hallowed ground for me.

My second visit to Ellora was with my right leg in a cast. I had fractured it days before a scheduled trip and true to my nature of refusing to back out of a trip, I decided to go anyway, with the assurance of my editor, Sudeshna, that she would accompany me and find ways to trundle me around. She kept her word, found wheelchairs in Ellora and a wheelchair assistant who was amazingly kind to me. Sanjayji pushed me up and down the caves and wherever needed held my hand as I hopped from stone to stone. He was a gem. Many thanks to this local friend.

Kailash was not easy to research. I read as many books I could lay my hands upon which were not many. *The Kailas at Ellora, New View of a Misunderstood Masterwork* by Roger Vogler, published by INTACH Aurangabad is a detailed study that I referred to and enjoyed reading.

The Penguin Guide To the Monuments of India, Volume 1 by George Michell is a fabulous text to get an overview of the chronology of events in Indian architecture. I dusted out Percy Brown's *Indian Architecture, Buddhist and Hindu Period*. This is such an oldie-but-goodie. Many of my references to the evolution of cave architecture was taken from this. *Ellora* by M. K. Dhavalkar is a great introduction to the caves and the evolution of this genre in India. I looked back a little on ancient civilizations and Yuval Noah Harari's *Sapiens* has always been an entertaining and enlightening read. And I read Amar Chitra Kathas for the myths of kings and battles which also gave me a visual context of a time long gone.

Historian and conservationist Swapna Liddle read the manuscript and gave invaluable advice on how to structure the book. She has encouraged me from the word go and I continue to be a fan of this scholar.

And of course, Ravi Singh, Publisher, Speaking Tiger, whose idea all this was has to be thanked. A reservoir of stories himself, Ravi, along with Sudeshna of Speaking Tiger have been people who have egged me on to read and write. Maithili Doshi laid out the pages spectacularly and I absolutely love the illustrations by Kavita Singh Kale. They adorn the pages which deserve the art as much as the words to truly illustrate the beauty of Kailash.

I hope this narrative of ancient India puts our history in perspective for the readers. I have attempted to make this book a narrative of our ancient history, albeit briefly. For young readers, this may be one of the few books on ancient Indian architecture and on the Kailash Temple. As always, history and conservation should be the gainers, once the story is known.

Picture Credits

Page 10, Daulatabad Fort, Wikimedia Commons
Page 11, Aurangzeb's tomb, Wikimedia Commons
Page 20, Great Bath, Mohenjodaro, Wikimedia Commons
Page 24, Sanchi Stupa, Wikimedia Commons
Page 27, Frescoes at Ajanta Caves, Vasukrishnan57, Wikimedia Commons
Page 28, Bhitargaon temple, Wikimedia Commons
Page 30, Ancient cave art, Wikimedia Commons
Page 31, Bhimbetka caves, Wikimedia Commons
Page 34, Chaitya hall, Kevin Standage, Wikimedia Commons
Page 37, Badami caves, Wikimedia Commons
Page 38, The chariots at Mahabalipuram, Wikimedia Commons
Page 39, Buddhist cave-temple, Wikimedia Commons
Page 40, Hindu cave-temple, Wikimedia Commons
Page 40, Jain cave-temple, Wikimedia Commons
Page 50-51, Virupaksha Temple, Kanchan Joshi, Wikimedia Commons
Page 53, Main entrance of Cave 16, Wikimedia Commons
Page 57, Temple with rock-cut hill, Sanket901, Wikimedia Commons
Page 68, Ravana shaking Kailash, photograph courtesy Robert Barnhill
Page 69, Sculptures at the entrance, Anupamg, Wikimedia Commons
Page 70, Gajalakshmi, Wikimedia Commons

Page 72, The River Goddess Complex, Wikimedia Commons

Page 74, Mahishasuramardini, Prashant1995, Wikimedia Commons

Page 75, Goddess Durga, Dipankan001, Wikimedia Commons

Page 77, North Court, photograph courtesy Robert Barnhill

Page 78, North Court with North Aisle, Aums90, Wikimedia Commons

Page 79, A skyscraper, Wikimedia Commons

Page 80, Lankeswara sculpture gallery, Dey.sandip, Wikimedia Commons

Page 82, Shiva dancing the tandava, Wikimedia Commons

Page 84, Rows of elephants, photograph courtesy Robert Barnhill

Page 85, Stone cantilever on East Aisle, Vyacheslav Argenberg, Wikimedia Commons

Page 89, Narasimha, Vu2sga, Wikimedia Commons

Page 92, Nandi bull, Saiiko, Wikimedia Commons

Page 93, View from above the gopuram, Nikita Rathore, https://www.sahapedia.org/kailash-temple-ellora-architectural-elements-and-shiva-sculptures#lg=1&slide=6

Page 94, The main hall, Runab WMF, Wikimedia Commons

Page 95, The inner sanctum, photograph courtesy Deepak Asthana

Page 96, Paintings on the ceiling, photograph courtesy Deepak Asthana

Page 97, Mahabharata panel, Sarah Welch, Wikimedia Commons

Page 99, Kailash complex, Archaeological Survey of India, Aurangabad Circle, https://asiaurangabadcircle.com/monuments/ellora/elloraCaves.php

Page 103, Ellora caves, Archaeological Survey of India, Aurangabad Circle, https://asiaurangabadcircle.com/monuments/ellora/elloraCaves.php

Page 106, Sanjay and me, Tilottama Shome

Page 110, Kailash Temple, Pratheeps, Wikimedia Commons

Also in the series

~ Magnificent Monuments of India ~

Taj Mahal

The Story of a Wonder of the World

By Tilottama Shome • Illustrated by Kavita Singh Kale

The incredible story of one of the Wonders of the World

In 1631, the empress Mumtaz Mahal died at childbirth, leaving her husband, the mighty emperor Shah Jahan, soaked in grief. Out of this sadness was born the idea of building a unique mausoleum or resting place for

Mumtaz Mahal. The Taj Mahal went on to be considered the most beautiful building in the world. It symbolized Shah Jahan's love for his wife, and was a statement of Mughal power and splendour.

In *Taj Mahal*, Tilottama Shome, an architect herself by training, lucidly narrates the story of the Mughal dynasty and how the Taj Mahal came to be built. Accompanied by detailed plans, maps, illustrations and photographs, it explains how the Taj was designed, the deep symbols that lie hidden everywhere in its plan, and the stories of the people who built it—from a mighty emperor, to renowned architects, to the humble stoneworkers and masons who worked on it for years.

As wonderful as it is moving, this beautifully designed book will educate young readers on their heritage, as well as inspire them to create and appreciate beauty for themselves.

Tilottama Shome is an architect by training and wanderer by profession. Curious about all things historical and old, she has travelled, or rather wandered in different countries, soaking in the local history, food, architecture and has friends all over the world.

Her interest in history and architecture and an inherent need to relate the stories of our buildings to the youth led her to write this series of books on Indian monuments. She sometimes took her two daughters along as she researched the monuments, exploring bat-infested caves and taking guided tours from a plethora of amusing storytellers.

Tilottama has also done translations from Bengali that have been published by Talking Cub and Pratham Books. She lives in Delhi.

An alumnus of National Institute of Design, Ahmedabad, and College of Art, Delhi University, Kavita Singh Kale has fifteen years of industry experience in broadcast design, children's content creation, animation film-making and transmedia art practice. Kavita has illustrated for a wide range of clients in adult and children's publishing. She is the co-founder of an interdisciplinary studio called Underground Worm Art & Design.

Also in the series:

Taj Mahal: The Story of a Wonder of the World